A Note to Parents and Teachers

Take a few moments to familiarize your child with his new dictionary before he uses it by himself. Acquaint him with the alphabetical pronunciation key at the beginning, with the categorized words pictured at the bottom of the large scenic spreads, and with the fact that each dictionary word is printed in special type in its sentence.

Show him how he can use the simplified pronunciation key. By matching the beginning sound of a word he is looking for with a key word in the list, he will know the beginning letter of his word and, therefore, the section of the book to turn to.

With a very brief familiarization, your child will get the most value from his dictionary. The preschool child will enjoy having parts read to him and discussing the relationship of the word and the picture. The school-age child will be able to use this dictionary as a spelling aid to writing. By using the key, he will gain valuable experience in listening for beginning sounds and readiness experience in using a reference tool. The thirteen large scenes provide interesting "picture reading" for the preschool child and ideas to write about for the beginning reader.

All words have been selected for this dictionary in terms of their frequency of use, based on the Horn, Rinsland, Thorndike, and Fitzgerald lists, as well as the Hillerich study (1965) of 380,000 words used by elementary-school children in creative writing. The total body of words represents over 75% of the words children most often use in their writing. Unlike most other beginning dictionaries, this dictionary does not limit itself to picturable words, but contains all high frequency words, including *the, is, was,* etc., because these words are essential to our language and, having no dictionary meaning as such, are the most difficult for children to learn to read and spell.

Robert L. Hillerich, Ed.D.

Rand McNally
Picturebook Dictionary

Illustrated by Dan Siculan

Compiled by

ROBERT L. HILLERICH, Ed.D.
MARVIN D. ENGLISH, Ph.D.
LUDWIG C. BODZEWSKI, M.A.
THEODORE C. KAMATOS, Ph.D.

National College of Education,
Graduate School,
Evanston, Illinois

 RAND MCNALLY & COMPANY   Chicago • New York • San Francisco

Copyright © 1971 by Rand McNally & Company. Cover copyright © 1982 by Rand McNally & Company.
All rights reserved. Printed in U.S.A.
Library of Congress Catalog Card Number: 79-157918. First printing, 1971. Second printing, 1982.

Simplified Pronunciation Key

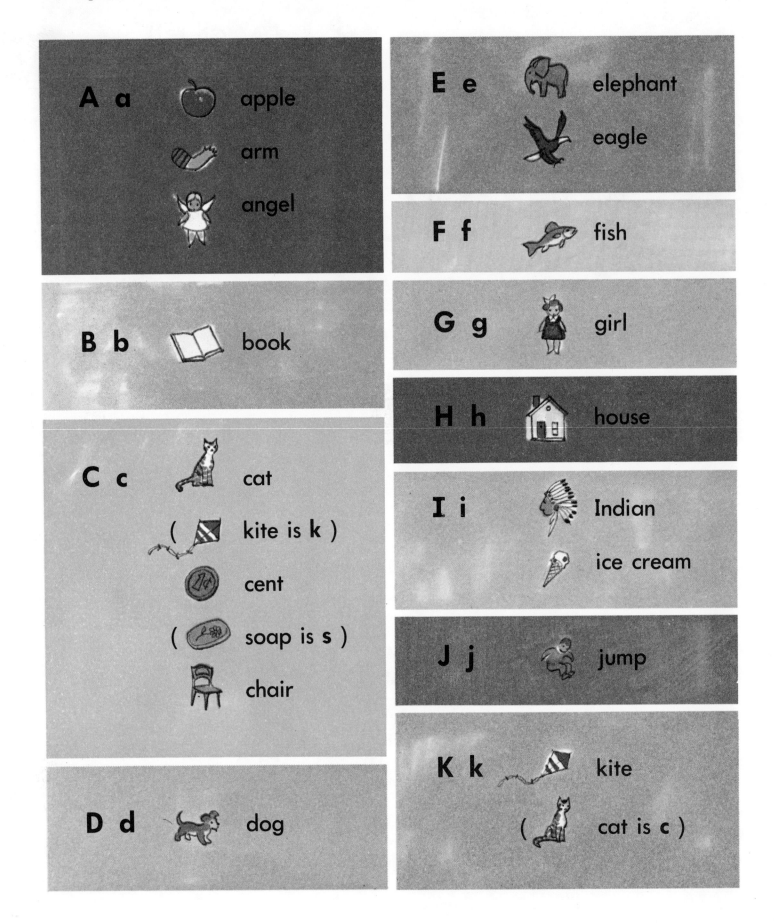

A a apple
arm
angel

B b book

C c cat
(kite is **k**)
cent
(soap is **s**)
chair

D d dog

E e elephant
eagle

F f fish

G g girl

H h house

I i Indian
ice cream

J j jump

K k kite
(cat is **c**)

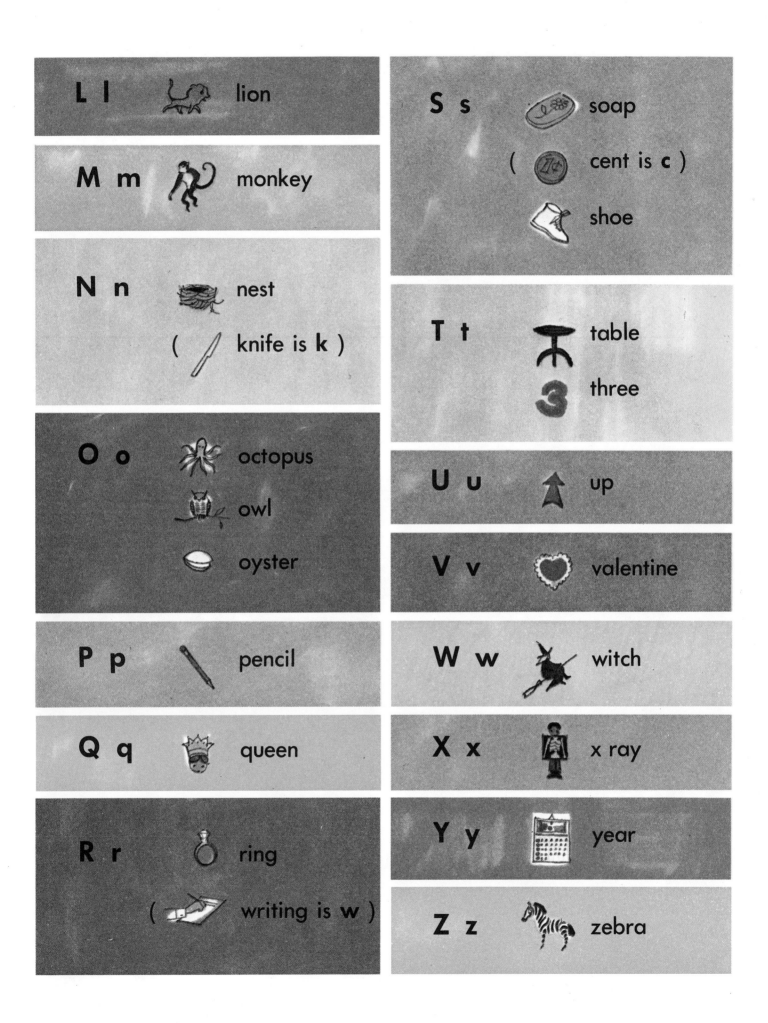

L l lion

M m monkey

N n nest

(knife is **k**)

O o octopus

owl

oyster

P p pencil

Q q queen

R r ring

(writing is **w**)

S s soap

(cent is **c**)

shoe

T t table

three

U u up

V v valentine

W w witch

X x x ray

Y y year

Z z zebra

Aa

a   The robin found **a** worm.

able   Older children are **able** to write their names.

about   John is **about** as tall as his sister.

above   An eagle flew **above** the trees.

across   A lost dog ran **across** the busy street.

act   It is fun to **act** in a play.
acts, acted, acting

add   **Add** yellow paint to blue to get green.
adds, added, adding

afraid   The pigs were not **afraid** of the big, bad wolf.

after   Mother did the dishes **after** lunch.

afternoon   In the **afternoon**, the teacher read a story.
afternoons

again The sun came out **again** from behind the clouds.

ahead Bob ran **ahead** of the other boys.

air We like to breathe cool, fresh **air.**

airplane Some people say "jet" instead of **airplane.**
airplanes

all **All** forest animals are afraid of fires.

almost It is **almost** time for lunch.

alone The kitten sat in her box, all **alone.**

along The boys walked **along** the stream.

already Ted had **already** put on his boots.

also Like his mother, the colt **also** had a white tail.

always Do clowns **always** look happy?

am I **am** drawing a picture of my teacher.

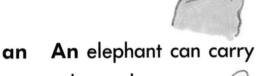

an **An** elephant can carry a heavy log.

and Gwen **and** her friends are playing leapfrog.

animal The aardvark is a funny **animal**.
animals

another Mary, here is **another** book about horses.

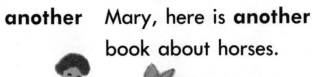

answer To **answer** the phone, Tim stands on a stool.
answers, answered, answering

any Morris does not have **any** marbles left.

apple Mary found a worm in her **apple**.
apples

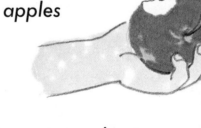

are "**Are** you a ghost or a goblin?"

arm   Father fixes
the doll's broken **arm**.
arms

around   **Around** and around
goes the merry-go-round.

as   **As** the sun rises,
the birds begin to sing.

ask   **Ask** Father to fix your wagon.
asks, asked, asking

asleep   The tired pup falls
asleep on Jane's lap.

at   The monkeys **at** the zoo
watch the people.

ate   The bear **ate** some berries
and waddled away.
eat, eats, eaten, eating

aunt   **Aunt** Kate is
my mother's sister.
aunts

away   The bird flew **away**
when the cat came near.

Bb

baby   **Baby** Bill is fat
and fun to play with.
babies

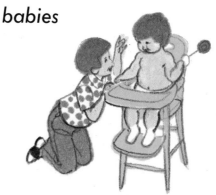

  tractor wagon

 truck gate

barn  cow

silo horse

pond  chicken

 pig

 corncrib

 colt

 duck

farmer

 calf

 rooster

fence

haystack

pasture

back The crab wears his house on his **back.**
backs

bad The truck hit a **bad** bump in the road.

bag Mother's shopping **bag** is full of groceries.
bags

ball Susan's **ball** bounces over her head.
balls

bark This little dog can **bark.**
barks, barked, barking

barn "There's a skunk in the **barn!**"
barns

basket Kittens in the **basket,** one, two, three.
baskets

bat John swung his **bat** very hard
bats

bath The twins have fun taking a **bath** together.
baths

be "**Be** careful when crossing streets!"
been

bear The little **bear** cub
likes honey.
bears

beat Jim **beat** John
in the potato sack race.
beats, beaten, beating

beautiful Indians can weave
beautiful blankets.

because Is a clown funny **because**
he has a big nose?

become Tom wants to **become**
an astronaut.
becomes, became, becoming

bed Mother cat looks for the
kitten under the **bed.**
beds

been "Where have you **been?"**
asks Mother.
be

before "Brush your teeth
before going to bed."

begin "Let's **begin** our race here."
*begins, began, begun,
beginning*

behind The elephant is hiding
behind a tree.

believe They **believe** there are ghosts in the house.
believes, believed, believing

bell The **bell** calls the campers to lunch.
bells

belong "Do these kittens **belong** to you?"
belongs, belonged, belonging

beside The little tug is **beside** the ocean liner.

better Two dolls are **better** than one.
good, best

between The cow runs **between** the rows of corn.

big "Cats are very **big**," says the mouse.
bigger, biggest

bike The clown's **bike** has crooked wheels.
bikes

bird A **bird** sits on the scarecrow's hat.
birds

birthday Tommy got a helicopter for his **birthday**.
birthdays

bite "That's a pretty big
bite, Sue."
bites

black Lucy has **black** paint
all over her dress.

blow "Little Boy Blue,
come **blow** your horn."
blows, blew, blown, blowing

blue White fluffy clouds float
in the **blue** sky.

boat "You'll get wet
in that leaky **boat.**"
boats

body The Indian paints stripes
on his **body.**
bodies

book Diane likes to carry
her father's big **book.**
books

born These three kittens
were **born** last night.

both **Both** of these girls
like hot dogs.

bowl Baby Bear's **bowl** is empty.
bowls

box Jim puts the big **box** over his head.
boxes

boy The **boy** pulls his sled up the hill.
boys

branch Betsy swings from a **branch** of a tree.
branches

bread Helen likes **bread** and peanut butter.

bright Hal shades his eyes from the **bright** sun.
brighter, brightest

brother Anna and her **brother** kiss their mother.
brothers

brown **Brown** squishy mud feels good on bare feet.

build Beavers **build** dams in the stream.
builds, built, building

burn The logs **burn** brightly in the fireplace.
burns, burned, burning

bus Sarah and her friends ride the school **bus**.
buses

busy   Mother is **busy** baking
gingerbread men.
busier, busiest

but   Walt put on his shoe,
but forgot the sock.

butter   Julie likes **butter**
on her popcorn.

buy   Don has enough money
to **buy** the balloon.
buys, bought, buying

by   Grandma says,
"Come, sit **by** me."

Cc

cake   The big piece of **cake**
is for Daddy.
cakes

call   Johnny likes to **call**
his Grandpa.
calls, called, calling

came   All of the ants **came**
to the picnic, too.
come, comes, coming

camp   Scouts are returning
to **camp** after a hike.
camps

can   "Look, I **can** turn
a cartwheel."
could

 flag

 toolbox

 wagon

  bike

 chair

 slide

 principal

 flowers

 book

 hammer

 custodian

 block

 boys

 children

teacher

 clock

 glasses

 girls

jungle gym

swing

candy   Cotton **candy** gets
all over your face.
candies

cap   The big **cap** comes down
over Sam's ears.
caps

car   The **car** in the circus
is full of clowns.
cars

card   "Look, Father,
my first library **card**!"
cards

care   Joan takes good **care**
of her hamster.

carry   It takes two boys
to **carry** the big box.
carries, carried, carrying

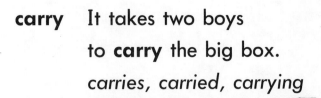

cat   The witch's **cat** rides
on her broomstick.
cats

catch   Can a seal **catch** a ball?
catches, caught, catching

catcher   The **catcher**
has his mask on.
catchers

chair   Father Bear's **chair**
was too hard.
chairs

change "Bill, go home and **change** your wet shoes." *changes, changed, changing*

chicken A baby **chicken** comes from an egg. *chickens*

chief The Indian **chief** smokes his peace pipe. *chiefs*

child The **child** rides the little pony. *children*

church In this **church**, there lives a little mouse. *churches*

circus The lion tamer works at the **circus**. *circuses*

city This **city** has tall buildings. *cities*

clean Skiers like the **clean** mountain snow. *cleaner, cleanest*

climb Ann likes to **climb** the monkey bars. *climbs, climbed, climbing*

clock This **clock** shakes when it rings. *clocks*

close "**Close** the gate to the tiger cage!"
closes, closed, closing

clothes "Will you please hang up your **clothes**!"
clothing

club Our **club** meets in this secret place.
clubs

coat Harry has ten buttons on his **coat**.
coats

cold It's **cold** enough to flood the ice rink.
colder, coldest

color The **color** of the doll buggy is pink.
colors

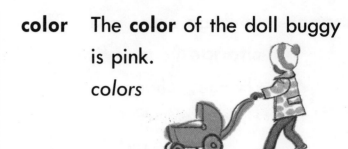

come "**Come** here and see what I have found."
comes, came, coming

company We have **company** for dinner.

cook Sue and her brother are learning to **cook**.
cooks, cooked, cooking

cookie Milk and a big **cookie** make a delicious snack.
cookies

cool   A snowman likes to keep **cool**.
cooler, coolest

corn   Who likes **corn** on the cob?

corner   The naughty puppy sits in the **corner**.
corners

cost   "How much do these skates **cost**?"
costs, cost, costing

could   I **could** ride a bike, too, if I had one.
can

country   In the **country**, Peg sees farms and forests.

cousin   Aunt Kate's son is Sue's **cousin**.
cousins

cover   We always **cover** the boat for the winter.
covers, covered, covering

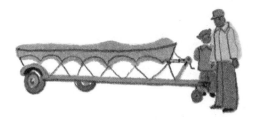

cow   The farmer's **cow** has a baby calf.
cows

cross   Boy scouts **cross** the rope bridge.
crosses, crossed, crossing

 bakery department

 basket

 bag

 box

 can

 cashier

check-out counter

 customer

 dairy department

 fruit

 frozen-food department

 fish

 ice cream

 meat

 milk

 money

 shelf

 showcase

vegetables

 worker

cry "Don't **cry**, Bill,
Dad will fix your toy."
cries, cried, crying

cup "Oh boy, a **cup**
of hot chocolate!"
cups

cut Carol wants to **cut**
her own birthday cake.
cuts, cutting

Dd

dad Eric and his **dad**
play ball on the beach.
dads

dance Mary likes to **dance**
and twirl to the music.
dances, danced, dancing

dark The man lights a match
in the **dark** cave.
darker, darkest

day The farmer's **day** begins
with the sunrise.
days

dear Daddy hugs the baby
and says, "**Dear** Pammy."
dearer, dearest

dig A steam shovel can **dig**
a deep hole.
digs, dug, digging

deer The **deer** is drinking water
from the stream.
deer

desk　There is a big, red apple on teacher's **desk**.
desks

did　"Freddie, **did** you wipe your shoes?"
do, does, done, doing

dinner　The family sits down to a turkey **dinner**.
dinners

dish　The waiter gives Tim a **dish** of ice cream.
dishes

do　**Do** frogs really play leapfrog?
does, did, done, doing

doctor　The **doctor** is listening to Jack's heart.
doctors

dog　King is a very big **dog**.
dogs

doll　This **doll** cries and wets her panties.
dolls

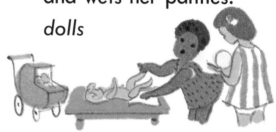

dollar　Jane got a **dollar** with her birthday card.
dollars

done　"When the lawn is **done**, put the mower away."
do, does, did, doing

door There's a goblin behind the **door.**
doors

down **Down** the slide comes the ski jumper.

draw **Draw** a clown juggling ten plates.
draws, drawn, drawing

dream Sugarplum fairies dance in Ann's **dream.**
dreams

dress Cinderella is beautiful in her new **dress.**
dresses

drink The sign says, "Do not **drink.**"
drinks, drank, drinking

drop "Don't **drop** the eggs!"
drops, dropped, dropping

dry Greg uses a big towel to **dry** himself.
dries, dried, drying

duck The **duck** sticks her head in the water.
ducks

during The children talk and laugh **during** lunch.

Ee

each   Mother gives **each**
of her children a kiss.

ear   The elephant's **ear**
looks like a big leaf.
ears

early   Father gets up **early**
to go fishing.
earlier, earliest

earth   The jet flies high
above the **earth**.

east   The sun rises in the **east**.

easy   Is it **easy** to catch
a greased pig?
easier, easiest

eat   John likes to **eat** watermelon.
eats, ate, eaten, eating

egg   The farmer puts another **egg**
into the basket.
eggs

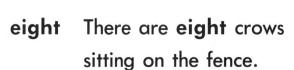

eight   There are **eight** crows
sitting on the fence.

else   "Wash behind your ears,
or **else** I will."

 squirrel

 robin

clouds

bushes

nest

blue jay

 snake

 mushroom

 beaver

 dam

 acorn hill

cattail

 stream frog forest ranger

violet

branch owl lookout tower

enjoy "I **enjoy** roller skating," says Father.

enjoys, enjoyed, enjoying

enough Mary Ellen has had **enough** chicken.

even "Here is your candy. That makes us **even**."

evening The moon and stars are out in the **evening**.

evenings

ever You will never **ever** see a horse in a suit.

every **Every** boy and girl should smile.

eye This boy is winking his **eye** at you.

eyes

Ff

face My little brother has a dirty **face**.

faces

fairy The happy **fairy** is on my windowsill.

fairies

fall The leaves are colorful in the **fall**.

fall   The squirrel is waiting
for a nut to **fall**.
falls, fell, fallen, falling

family   The Bear **family** has a
Mama, Papa, and Baby bear.
families

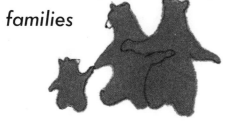

far   The moon is **far** away
from the earth.
farther, farthest

farm   Cows and pigs
live on a **farm**.
farms

fat   This is a **fat** cat.
fatter, fattest

father   **Father** Bear sits
in a big chair.
fathers

feed   Children **feed** the birds
in winter.
feeds, fed, feeding

feel   Sue likes to **feel**
her fluffy teddy bear.
feels, felt, feeling

fence   The boys peek
through the **fence**.
fences

few   The man has only
a **few** balloons left.
fewer, fewest

field The boys play ball in a **field.**
fields

fifty **Fifty** is a large number.

fight A cat and a dog will sometimes **fight.**
fights, fought, fighting

fill Tom likes to **fill** the tub with water.
fills, filled, filling

find Billy can't **find** his glove.
finds, found, finding

fine Some sand is coarse, but some is as **fine** as sugar.
finer, finest

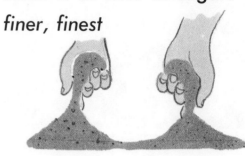

finger Here is a **finger** puppet.
fingers

fire Four firemen fought the **fire.**
fires

first The **first** book is taller.

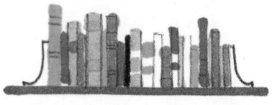

fish Funny Fred caught a **fish** in a bucket.
fishes

five   Here are **five** pieces of bubble gum.

flat   If you sit on your lunch, it will be **flat**.
flatter, flattest

floor   Mary sweeps the **floor** every morning.
floors

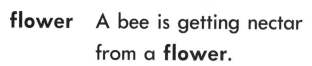

flower   A bee is getting nectar from a **flower**.
flowers

fly   A kite can **fly** high in the sky.
flies, flew, flown, flying

follow   Ants **follow** each other in a line.
follows, followed, following

food   The **food** is on the picnic table.
foods

foot   Ted can hop on one **foot**.
feet

for   Here is a letter **for** you.

forest   Rabbits and squirrels like the **forest**.
forests

four **Four** fingers fit here.

fox A **fox** in a box
is funny to see.
foxes

free What a day it would be
if candy were **free**.

friend Happiness is having
a **friend**.
friends

from Tommy got a truck
from Uncle Charlie.

front The engine is at the **front**
of the train.

full Jack ate so much, he is **full**.
fuller, fullest

fun Boys and girls have **fun**
at the circus.

funny Here is a **funny** clown.
funnier, funniest

fur People can wear
fur coats, too.
furry

Gg

game   Tag is a good **game** to play.
games

get   Dad and Mary **get** to ride the motorcycle.
gets, got, gotten, getting

girl   Miss Muffet is the **girl** who sat on a tuffet.
girls

give   Rob likes to **give** peanuts to the monkeys.
gives, gave, given, giving

glad   Pedro was **glad** to see his friend.

glass   This cat drinks milk from a **glass.**
glasses

go   The green light tells us to **go.**
goes, gone, went, going

gold   Pirates kept **gold** in their treasure chests.

gone   Baby Bear found his porridge was **gone.**

good   Chocolate is **good** on ice cream.
better, best

SEPTEMBER

SUN	MON	TUE	WED	THU	FRI	SAT
			1	2	3	4
5	6	7	8	9	10	11
12	13	14	15	16	17	18
19	20	21	22	23	24	25
26	27	28	29	30		

10 years in 1 decade ⧗ 100 years in 1 century

24 hours in 1 day ⧗ 365 days in 1 year

60 seconds in 1 minute ⧗ 60 minutes in 1 hour

ANNUAL TIME PARADE

1 o'clock   4 o'clock   7 o'clock   10 o'clock

2 o'clock   5 o'clock   8 o'clock   11 o'clock

3 o'clock   6 o'clock   9 o'clock   12 o'clock

1, one, first

2, two, second

3, three, third

4, four, fourth

5, five, fifth

6, six, sixth

7, seven, seventh

8, eight, eighth

9, nine, ninth

10, ten, tenth

grass Billy forgot to mow the **grass**.

green Jerry found a **green** snake.

ground Tom's airplane crashed to the **ground**.

grow Plant a seed and watch it **grow**.
grows, grew, grown, growing

guess **Guess** what is in the box.
guesses, guessed, guessing

gun Even a toy **gun** can hurt someone.
guns

Hh

had Alice **had** an ice-cream cone.
has, have, having

hair Rapunzel let down her **hair** for the prince.

half Someone cut this apple in **half**.
halves

Halloween We dress up like witches on **Halloween**.

hand   Debby holds on
to her Daddy's **hand**.
hands

hang   We saw a monkey **hang**
by his tail.
hangs, hung, hanging

happen   John saw an accident
happen at the corner.
*happens, happened,
happening*

happy   A smiling face
is a **happy** face.
happier, happiest

hard   Grass is soft
but the sidewalk is **hard**.
harder, hardest

has   Tommy **has** a fly on his nose.
have, had, having

have   Joe and Jim **have**
a tree house.
has, had, having

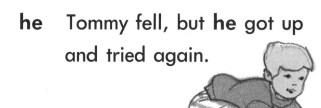

he   Tommy fell, but **he** got up
and tried again.

head   The **head** of our turtle
is sticking out.
heads

hear   Colleen can **hear**
the big brass band.
hears, heard, hearing

heart Mother has a **heart** on her valentine.
hearts

help Joey is going to **help** Dad dry the dishes.
helps, helped, helping

her Laurie pulls his wagon with **her** bike.
hers

hide Ann is trying to **hide** in the clothes basket.
hides, hid, hidden, hiding

high "How **high** can you swing?"
higher, highest

hill Tom likes to slide down a **hill**.
hills

him Mary is giving **him** a ball.

hit Tom **hit** the ball over the fence.
hits, hit, hitting

hold It's not easy to **hold** a wet fish.
holds, held, holding

hole Big or small, a **hole** is fun to dig.
holes

home Harry ran all the way **home** in the rain.
homes

hope "I **hope** the cake is good," says Jill.
hopes, hoped, hoping

horse The Indian rides a pinto **horse**.
horses

hot The **hot** sand burns Candy's bare feet.
hotter, hottest

hour Sometimes an **hour** seems like a long time.
hours

house This is the **house** that Jack built.
houses

how "**How** does the magician do that trick?"

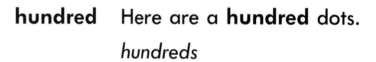

hundred Here are a **hundred** dots.
hundreds

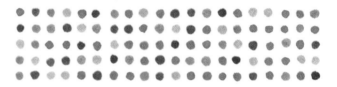

hunt Jerry likes to **hunt** for seashells.
hunts, hunted, hunting

hurt "Careful, Bill, don't **hurt** the kitty."
hurts, hurt, hurting

Ii

I   Sally says, "I have a blue balloon."

ice   Sam put **ice** cubes in the lemonade.

ice cream   "Give me two scoops of **ice cream**, please."

if   There would be lots of pets **if** it rained cats and dogs.

in   Jack is **in** the box.

Indian   This **Indian** is a chief.
Indians

instead   Boy Blue slept in the hay **instead** of his bed.

into   The train is going **into** the tunnel.

is   "You're right, Fred, it really **is** a snake."

it   John caught a cricket, but **it** got away.

Jj

jet A **jet** is a very fast plane.
jets

joy Great is the **joy**
of a boy with a toy.
joys

jump Katie and Colin
can **jump** rope very well.
jumps, jumped, jumping

just Lift it up
just a little higher.

Kk

keep Sally likes to **keep**
snowballs in the freezer.
keeps, kept, keeping

kind Fred doesn't know which
kind of candy to buy.
kinds

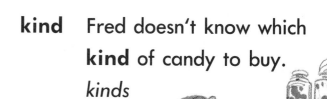

king The **king** wears a
crown of gold.
kings

kiss Don't forget to **kiss**
Mom and Dad good-night.
kisses, kissed, kissing

kitchen We all made popcorn
in the **kitchen.**
kitchens

kitten A little **kitten** is
playing with string.
kittens

 allosaurus

 brontosaurus

 **stegosaurus**

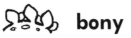 **bony armor**

 foliage

 palm tree

 fern

 skeleton

 **pterodactyl**

 swamp

 bones

 claws

 volcano

 tail

 lizard

 triceratops

 tyrannosaurus

 diplodocus

know   Tom doesn't **know** where he left his ball.

knows, knew, known, knowing

Ll

lady   The **lady** has on a big hat.

ladies

lake   The boats are racing on the **lake**.

lakes

land   It's fun to watch the jets **land**.

lands, landed, landing

large   Patty made a snowman as **large** as she is.

larger, largest

last   Z is the **last** letter of the alphabet.

late   Joe is **late** for dinner.

later, latest

lay   **Lay** the wet paintings on the floor to dry.

lays, laid, laying

learn   Can a puppy **learn** to jump through a hoop?

learns, learned, learning

leave   The family has to **leave** the dog at home.

leaves, left, leaving

left   Luis is holding up his **left** hand.

leg   A flamingo sleeps on one **leg**.

legs

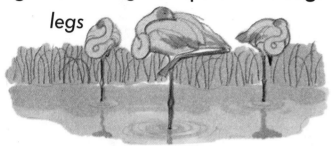

let   Dan **let** his little sister ride in the wagon.

lets, let, letting

letter   The mailman is bringing a **letter** for Linda.

letters

lie   The kids **lie** on the floor to watch TV.

lies, lay, lain, lying

like   "Do you really **like** pickles and ice cream?"

likes, liked, liking

line   It's fun to draw a wiggly **line**.

lines

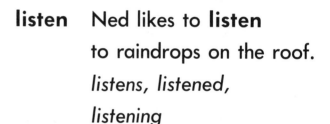

listen   Ned likes to **listen** to raindrops on the roof.

listens, listened, listening

little   A toy poodle is a **little** dog.

littler, littlest

live   Two raccoons **live** in the tree.

lives, lived, living

long   Old English sheep dogs have **long** hair.
longer, longest

look   It's good to **look** where you are going.
looks, looked, looking

lot   Mike has a **lot** of mustard on his hot dog.
lots

love   The girls **love** to go up on the swing.
loves, loved, loving

low   A dachshund's tummy is almost as **low** as a snake's.
lower, lowest

lunch   Pete carries his **lunch** to school in a box.
lunches

Mm

mail   Here comes the truck with the **mail**.

make   Daddy is helping Sam **make** a snowman.
makes, made, making

man   This **man** brings milk to our house.
men

marry   Bill is seeing his sister **marry** John.
marries, married, marrying

may   Mother says we **may** play
in the rain.
might

me   Sherri always says,
"Let **me** do it!"

mean   Joe didn't **mean** to step
on his brother's toe.
means, meant, meaning

meat   Ted likes a lot of **meat**
for dinner.
meats

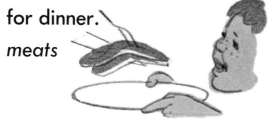

meet   Sylvia is happy to **meet**
a new friend.
meets, met, meeting

middle   The cat in the **middle**
is Blackie.

might   "Careful, that **might** be
thin ice!"
may

mile   The crooked man walked
a crooked **mile**.
miles

milk   **Milk** is good to drink.

mind   Sally doesn't **mind**
taking care of her puppy.
minds, minded

 airplane

 airport

 automobile

 barge

 bicycle

canal

expressway

 harbor

 helicopter

 highway

 motorcycle

 pipeline

 railroad

 ship

 subway

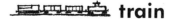 train

 truck

 tunnel

 bridge

 taxi

mine The bat is yours, but the ball is **mine**.

miss Dan is going to **miss** the target again.
misses, missed, missing

money Steve likes to put his **money** in his bank.

month January is the first **month** of the year.
months

moon A rocket ship can go to the **moon**.
moons

more Dad has **more** pockets than Jim.
much, most

morning The rooster crows in the **morning**.
mornings

most Which has the **most** legs?
much, more

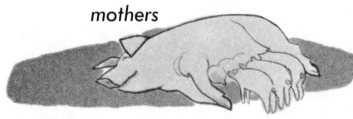

mother This **mother** pig has three piglets.
mothers

mountain Can you ski down this high **mountain**?
mountains

mouse   This little **mouse**
likes cheese.
mice

move   Jenny is too little
to **move** the big wagon.
moves, moved, moving

Mr.   **Mr.** Smith is a friend
of my father.

Mrs.   The lady at the door
is **Mrs.** Jones.

much   This cup holds as **much**
as the glass.
more, most

music   Jack plays **music**
on his violin.

must   Peter Piper **must** like
pickled peppers.

my   Tom says, "This is not
my coat."

Nn

name   This dog's **name** is Heidi.
names

near   Don't stand too **near**
the lion's cage.
nearer, nearest

need Kathy will **need** money
to buy ice cream.
needs, needed, needing

nest Two eggs are
in the robin's **nest**.
nests

never They **never** put Humpty
Dumpty together again.

new Jerry's **new** shoes squeak.
newer, newest

next Mary is **next** in line
after John.

night Owls like to fly
at **night**.
nights

nine There are **nine** boats
in the race.

no Goldilocks found **no** bears
at home.

noise A horn makes **noise**.
noises

north Geese fly **north**
in the spring.

nose The elephant has the longest **nose** of all.
noses

not Do **not** talk with your mouth full.

note Dad is writing a **note** to Mother.
notes

nothing There is **nothing** to eat in the basket.

now **Now** we can go out in the rain.

Oo

o'clock School is over at three **o'clock**.

of The tree house is made **of** wood.

off The sign says, "Keep **off** the grass."

KEEP OFF THE GRASS

often Mary goes swimming **often**.

old Is there a ghost in that **old** house?
older, oldest

on   Indians **on** horseback
are chasing buffalo.

once   I **once** saw
a shooting star.

one   Susie is hopping
on **one** leg.

only   There's **only** one cookie
left in the jar.

open   Fluffy can **open** the door
with his nose.
opens, opened, opening

or   "Tom, do you want an apple
or a peach?"

other   Irving lost
the **other** mitten.
others

our   **Our** dog is the furry one.

out   Some fish jump **out**
of the water.

over   Jack jumped **over**
the candlestick.

own We **own** that boat
on the beach.
owns, owned, owning

Pp

paint Tom likes to **paint**
at the easel.
paints, painted, painting

pair Which two mittens
make a **pair**?
pairs

paper Janie likes to cut out
paper dolls.
papers

park The jungle gym
is in the **park**.
parks

part This airplane has
one **part** missing.
parts

party Sue has a new dress
for the **party**.
parties

pass Please **pass** the pickles.
passes, passed, passing

pay Davy is going to **pay**
for the pony ride.
pays, paid, paying

pen This new **pen** writes
even underwater.
pens

 red

 **blue**

 **yellow**

 **purple**

green

 **orange**

 mouth

teeth

 shoulder

chin

elbow

 wrist

thumb

 stomach

knee

ankle

pencil Bill sharpened his **pencil** too much.
pencils

pet A **pet** can be a good friend.
pets

pick We **pick** apples from a tree.
picks, picked, picking

picnic The park is a great place for a **picnic**.
picnics

picture Mother is taking a **picture** of Tommy.
pictures

pie Which piece of **pie** would you take?
pies

piece One **piece** is missing from the puzzle.
pieces

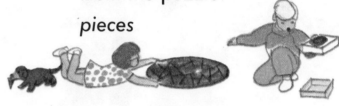

pin Can Amy **pin** the tail on the donkey?
pins, pinned, pinning

place Tim is saving Sam's **place** in the line.
places

plain Some cookies are fancy and some are **plain**.
plainer, plainest

plane This **plane** is taking off.
planes

plant We **plant** seeds
to see them grow.
plants, planted, planting

play Do you like to **play** games
at recess?
plays, played, playing

please "**Please** play
jacks with me."

point **Point** to the puppy
you like best.
points, pointed, pointing

pond Croaking frogs live
in the muddy **pond**.
ponds

pony A playful **pony** pranced
around the ring.
ponies

pool The seals keep cool
in the **pool**.
pools

poor **Poor** Jack,
he missed the bus.
poorer, poorest

pretty Can a chimpanzee paint
a **pretty** picture?
prettier, prettiest

pull   Two horses can hardly **pull** this wagon.
pulls, pulled, pulling

puppy   The frisky **puppy** is chasing the ball.
puppies

put   Jenny can **put** her nose up to the window.
puts, put, putting

Qq

question   The **question** is written on the blackboard.
questions

WHAT HAS FOUR LEGS AND CAN'T RUN?

quite   Tom is not **quite** as tall as Peter.

Rr

rabbit   This hungry **rabbit** is eating our carrots.
rabbits

race   Who won the **race**, the tortoise or the hare?
races

rain   **Rain**, rain, go away, let the sun shine today!

rather   I'd **rather** play dress-up than anything else.

reach   Can you **reach** the cookie jar on the shelf?
reaches, reached, reaching

read Fritz can **read** a book
all by himself.
reads, read, reading

ready The rocket is **ready**
for liftoff.

red Let's all ride
on the big **red** bus.

remember Jerry tries to **remember**
where his lunch is.
*remembers, remembered,
remembering*

rest "It's time to **rest**,"
says the scout leader.
rests, rested, resting

ride "**Ride** him, cowboy!"
rides, rode, ridden, riding

right Bob throws a ball
with his **right** hand.

ring Sue's prize was a shiny **ring**.
rings

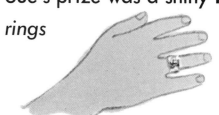

river They are paddling
a canoe down the **river**.
rivers

road Which is the right **road**
to follow?
roads

 street

 car

 school bus

 driveway

 pool

 sprinkler

hose

 bush

flowers

 tree

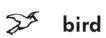 **bird**

 **tree house**

 lawn mower

roof

 chimney

 mailbox

garage

 window

 patio

 **grill**

robin This **robin** is feeding
her babies.
robins

rock The elf hid
behind a big **rock**.
rocks

roll We **roll** little snowballs
into big snowmen.
rolls, rolled, rolling

room There is a pillow fight
in Becky's **room**.
rooms

rope The cowboy lassoed
the steer with his **rope**.
ropes

rose A red **rose**
is a pretty flower.
roses

round Which balloon
is the **round** one?

rubber Nancy can bounce
the **rubber** ball.

rug Daddy is putting a **rug**
on the floor.
rugs

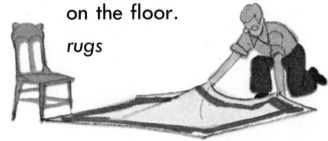

run A cheetah can **run** faster
than almost anything.
runs, ran, running

Ss

said "Frogs are fun," **said** Fred.

says, say, saying

salt Mother is putting **salt** in the shaker.

same Jack and Bill play on the **same** team.

sand Wendy is shaking the **sand** out of her shoe.

save Lifeguards **save** people from drowning.

saves, saved, saving

saw The class **saw** a play in school.

sees, see, seen, seeing

say Irving doesn't like to **say** good-bye.

says, said, saying

school Our **school** has a big playground.

schools

sea A submarine can sail under the **sea.**

seas

seat Joan's **seat** in school is near the window.

seats

second The giraffe is **second** in the parade.

see Jan can **see** a squirrel up in the tree.
sees, saw, seen, seeing

seed A **seed** needs water and sunlight to grow.
seeds

seen The ostrich thinks he can't be **seen**.
see, sees, saw, seeing

sell Tony digs up worms to **sell** to fishermen.
sells, sold, selling

send Sailors **send** messages with flags.
sends, sent, sending

set Dick has a new train **set**.
sets

seven **Seven** shiny seals sat on the sand.

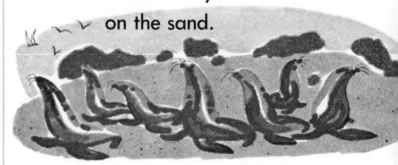

shall I **shall** listen with both ears.
should

she **She** is our neighbor and visits us often.

sheep   The man is shearing the **sheep.**
sheep

ship   The **ship** is being pushed by tugboats.
ships

shoe   Jack is learning to tie his **shoe.**
shoes

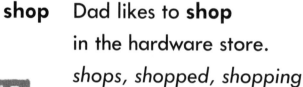

shop   Dad likes to **shop** in the hardware store.
shops, shopped, shopping

shore   The boys are rowing to **shore.**
shores

short   Our funny puppy has a **short** tail.
shorter, shortest

should   Donna **should** have worn her raincoat.
shall

show   Let me **show** you my secret hideout.
shows, showed, shown, showing

sick   The veterinarian takes care of **sick** pets.
sicker, sickest

side   Bruce and Jean stood **side** by side.
sides

 giraffe

 lion

 elephant

 lioness

 cub

water hole

 gazelle

carcass

 zebra

 tracks

rhinoceros

hippopotamus

anteater

vine

gorilla

vulture

monkey

orchid

python

crocodile

since You have grown **since** your last visit.

sing Campers **sing** around a campfire.
sings, sang, sung, singing

sister My **sister** is the one with the pigtails.
sisters

sit "Don't **sit** on the park bench."
sits, sat, seated, sitting

six **Six** is half a dozen.

skate It's fun to **skate** around the pond.
skates, skated, skating

skin This snake is shedding its **skin**.
skins

sky Jerry sees the lightning in the dark **sky**.
skies

sled The **sled** went over a bump.
sleds

sleep Bats **sleep** upside down.
sleeps, slept, sleeping

slide   "Whee-ee! See him **slide**!"
slides, slid, sliding

small   Elephants think people
are very **small**.
smaller, smallest

snow   You can walk on **snow**
with snowshoes.

so   Ted was **so** tired,
he fell asleep.

soap   We wash with **soap** and water.

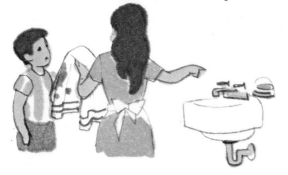

soft   Mama Bear's bed was too **soft**.
softer, softest

some   **Some** clowns are happy,
and some are sad.

song   The cat is singing
a good-night **song**.
songs

soon   How **soon** will the hot dogs
be ready?

sorry   Dan was **sorry** he broke
the window.
sorrier, sorriest

sound   Do you like the **sound** of bagpipes?

south   Some butterflies fly **south** for the winter.

space   Tom wants to explore outer **space**.

spell   Does Pedro know how to **spell** cat?
spells, spelled, spelling

spend   Karen has a dollar to **spend** for a gift.
spends, spent, spending

spring   Bears wake up in the **spring**.

squirrel   This smart **squirrel** is storing acorns.
squirrels

stand   Can you **stand** on your head?
stands, stood, standing

star   The evening **star** is the first to be seen.
stars

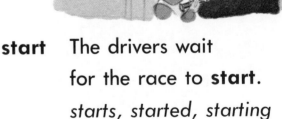

start   The drivers wait for the race to **start**.
starts, started, starting

stay How long can the cowboy **stay** on the bronco?
stays, stayed, staying

step Joan tried to **step** over the puddle.
steps, stepped, stepping

stick Dick has a **stick** for roasting hot dogs.
sticks

still Sit very **still** and watch the deer.

stone A **stone** is in Peter's shoe.
stones

stop We are waiting for the rain to **stop**.
stops, stopped, stopping

store Mom and Dad are shopping at the **store**.
stores

storm The big **storm** blew down the big tree.
storms

story Bob tells a scary **story** to the campers.
stories

stove This **stove** has four burners.
stoves

 downspout

 moving van

 crossing guard

 TV antenna

 stairs

 smoke

 mailbox

 hydrant

 street light

 skyscraper

 boulevard

 mailman

 manhole cover

 traffic light

puddle

 curb

 garbage truck

 fire escape

 doorway

 sidewalk

street The city workers are fixing the **street**.
streets

string John needs a ball of **string** to fly his kite.
strings

strong **Strong** horses pull the big circus wagon.
stronger, strongest

suddenly **Suddenly** it began to pour.

suit Johnny has a new **suit** of clothes.
suits

summer It is hot in the **summer**.

sun The poor snowman is melting in the **sun**.
suns

supper The family eats **supper** together.
suppers

sure Kathy was **sure** she could eat two hot dogs.

surprise Grandmother's visit is a **surprise**.
surprises

sweet Roasted marshmallows taste very **sweet**.
sweeter, sweetest

swim Fish **swim** by wiggling their tails.
swims, swam, swimming

swing Gail likes to **swing** high in the sky.
swings, swung, swinging

Tt

table A **table** has four legs but can't run.
tables

tail Ted's kite needs a long **tail**.
tails

take "**Take** Daddy's hand when you skate."
takes, took, taken, taking

talk My sister likes to **talk** on the telephone.
talks, talked, talking

tall Stilts will make you **tall**.
taller, tallest

teach Dad will **teach** me how to catch a ball.
teaches, taught, teaching

teacher My **teacher** plays basketball with us.
teachers

tell   Jim can **tell**
a spooky story.
tells, told, telling

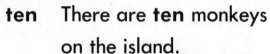

ten   There are **ten** monkeys
on the island.

than   A rabbit has longer ears
than a chipmunk.

thank   Joe says, "**Thank** you
for the nice present."
thanks, thanked, thanking

that   This bike is mine.
That one is yours.

the   **The** merry-go-round
is fun to ride.

their   Gladys and Marsha
missed **their** school bus.

them   "Here are my glasses.
I found **them**."

then   The seesaw goes up,
then it goes down.

there   Can you jump from
here to **there**?

these **These** boots are much too big.
those

they When the bell rings, **they** run to the fire engine.

thin The ice was too **thin**.
thinner, thinnest

thing We didn't leave a **thing** at the campground.
things

think Can you **think** of her name?
thinks, thought, thinking

third Tom is the **third** boy from the left.

this "No, come here and look at **this** one."

those **Those** boys are on our team.
these

thought Molly **thought** you were in there.
think, thinks, thinking

three Jeff can juggle **three** balls at one time.

 candy

 ice cream

 candles

 cake

prizes

 game

 ribbon

 present

 table

 chair

 plate

 cup

fork

spoon

clothespin

bottle

camera

balloon

 streamers

 napkins

through Crawl **through** my legs.

throw Always **throw** trash in the litter basket.
throws, threw, thrown, throwing

tie The fisherman will **tie** his boat to the dock.
ties, tied, tying

time Will Jim tell when it's **time** to leave?
times

tire The clowns have a flat **tire** on their car.
tires

to Let's run **to** the tree and back.

today **Today,** Larry is four years old.

together Les and Sarah are baking cookies **together.**

told Judy **told** Grace a secret.
tell, tells, telling

tomorrow We're going on our vacation **tomorrow.**

tonight   Let's catch lightning bugs **tonight**.

too   Daddy is **too** tired to play.

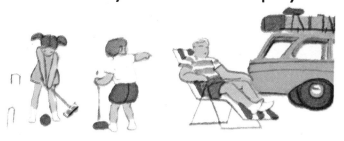

took   That dog **took** my lunch.
take, takes, taken, taking

top   The mountain climbers reached the **top**.
tops

town   Prairie dogs built a **town** in the desert.
towns

toy   Which **toy** does Peter want?
toys

trade   Mary will **trade** sandwiches with Jane.
trades, traded, trading

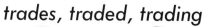

train   Mr. Jones is running to catch the **train**.
trains

tree   Whose cat is in that **tree**?
trees

trip   "Good-bye, we're going on a **trip**."
trips

trouble   Our puppy always gets into **trouble**.
troubles

truck   Ned's **truck** has real lights on it.
trucks

try   "Oops, you had better **try** it again."
tries, tried, trying

turn   **Turn** over the rock and look for worms.
turns, turned, turning

two   Mother thought we had only **two** rabbits.

Uu

uncle   **Uncle** Jack is Daddy's brother.
uncles

under   Tom's boat went **under** the bridge.

until   "Wait **until** Timmy catches up."

up   Jack and Jill went **up** the hill.

us   "This puppy just followed **us** home."

use George knows how to **use** a saw.
uses, used, using

Vv

very This is a **very** big hot dog.

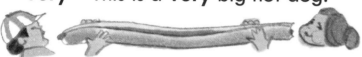

visit How many places is Betty going to **visit**?
visits, visited, visiting

Ww

wait People **wait** on the corner for the bus.
waits, waited, waiting

walk "Oh, a skunk! Let's quietly **walk** away."
walks, walked, walking

wall The wrecking crew knocked down the **wall**.
walls

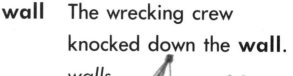

want Does Mother **want** popcorn, too?
wants, wanted, wanting

warm Carolyn's snowsuit is soft and **warm**.
warmer, warmest

was The frog **was** really the prince.
were

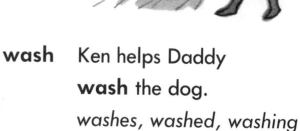

wash Ken helps Daddy **wash** the dog.
washes, washed, washing

watch **Watch** Katie
do a cartwheel.
watches, watched, watching

water It's fun to ski
on the **water**.

way Some streets go
only one **way**.
ways

we **We** are painting the fence.

wear When it is cold,
children **wear** snowsuits.
wears, wore, worn, wearing

week Daddy's vacation starts
next **week**.
weeks

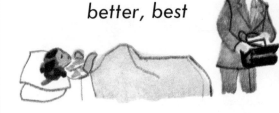

well The doctor says Karen
is getting **well**.
better, best

went Little Red Riding Hood
went into Granny's house.
go, goes, gone, going

were The tracks show
that bears **were** here.
was

wet Tom gets **wet** running
through the sprinkler.
wetter, wettest

what   **What** is in that cave?

when   I want to be a fireman **when** I grow up.

where   **Where** is Jimmy hiding?

which   **Which** dress shall I put on?

while   Will you hold the ladder **while** I climb?

whose   **Whose** smile is the happiest?

why   "**Why** are you puffing so hard?"

will   The dog **will** bring back the stick.
would

win   Our team wants to **win** the trophy.
wins, won, winning

wind   The **wind** blows Tina's hair in her face.
winds

 astronaut

 control center

 gantry

 life-support package

 nose cone

 launch pad

 radar tracking station

 rocket

 space suit

 van

 capsule

 **craters**

 earth

 instruments

 **lunar module**

 moon rock

 space ship

 parachute

 recovery ship

 last stage

window "Oh, oh, Billy broke the **window!**"
windows

winter I slide on my sled in the **winter.**

wish Did you ever make a **wish** at a wishing well?
wishes

with Jane's doll always goes **with** her.

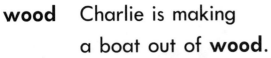

wood Charlie is making a boat out of **wood.**
woods

word That **word** means it's okay to cross the street.
words

work Sometimes I **work** with my Daddy.
works, worked, working

world He is a stranger to our **world.**
worlds

would "**Would** you like to play follow the leader?"
will

write Dick is trying to **write** his name.
writes, wrote, written, writing

wrong   "Oops, we took the **wrong** turn."

X ray   The **X ray** showed the broken bone.
X rays

yard   Jim plays with his puppy in his **yard**.
yards

year   Winter is the coldest time of the **year**.
years

yes   All who want to go on a picnic say, "**Yes!**"

yesterday   The puddles are from the rain **yesterday**.

yet   "Climb some more. We're not to the top **yet**."

you   They are bringing presents for **you**.

young   These ducklings are very **young**.
younger, youngest

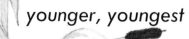

your   These are **your** friends.

zoo   Animals from many lands live in our **zoo**.
zoos